Find Me

In The

In-between

By Josie Eckersley *Josie*

To Brewlab

I wrote this in my favourite
armchair by the window!

Thankyou for the coffee
and company

9.01.24

Find Me In The In-between
Copyright © 2023
Josie Eckersley
First Edition

Book design by Josie Eckersley and Gemma Wong
ISBN 978-1-3999-6522-4

To everyone who is

hopeful and hopeless

at the same time.

Contents

<u>Part I</u>

The Past
is a familiar feeling,
something we can never really let go of,
the healing process is over
and what has happened
is cemented in your history.

There's never a day where you wake up
and magically become free.

It's a constant that's always there,
someday I'll be there too
If I'm not already.

We were always taught never to play with fire,
but why did our parents never warn us
that it wasn't the flames,
they were talking about?

The idea
that they still own her
never really escapes.

Bound to a soul,
that had no intention
of keeping their promises

and all they did was take and take her innocence.

- A story that sounds all too familiar.

I tell myself;

stop romanticising the trauma
that brought you here.

If it was a gift
then why do you cry at night
holding onto the string?

Losing friends
that gave you midnight memories,
hurts more when they become
just stories
because I hosted parties
just to see if they would
remember me.

Darling, if only you knew
the person I am now.

Forget the memories
and forget our past somehow,
and don't look at me with those scared eyes
thinking I'm the monster
from your dreams in disguise.

I'm not the girl I once was
the girl who fell from trees,
scraping her knees, playing in the leaves.

You have to understand
I'm not your version of me anymore.
I'm not the one showing up at your front door,
with my hand on my chest
and my heart on my sleeve,
and seeing your amazement and disbelief
that I'm making some grand
love gesture with a stereo,
you have to remember
that happened a long time ago.

I'm not the victim of your story
you forget so easily
that I'm not your territory.

Find Me In The In-between

I'm not the girl who tries to know how to fly,
knowing all she wants to do is try
when she can barely put one foot
in front of the other.

She wanted to be lost with you under the covers,
whispering about the future and lost causes
looking at you, wanting to kiss you

but pauses

because you once were
everything she ever wanted,
but now you're fading like a ghost
keeping her haunted.

I'm not the girl who always tried to save you
but even after everything you put me through,
I forgive you,
I learn to accept the past for what it is
reminding myself 'I'm no longer his'.

There's no need to feel sorry for me anymore,
because I know that you do.

I know that you are ok
and that taught me to be ok too.

Funny how we were told as children
that the monsters
were under our beds
not in them.

Find Me In The In-between

He can't be the monster under your bed
and the one you welcome into it.

He can't be your knight in shining armour
and the dragon keeping you in cages,
your memory brings it all back in stages.

A knife that frees
and also makes the marks,
you have to remember
you can't have the light without the dark.
The heavens without the hell,
your voice that can soothe
and burn me so well.

Which leads me to offer one last word,
that counters everything you've ever heard.

I could hold someone to the highest ideals,
whoever the murderer, the victim always feels

because no matter who I fall for or what I do,

I always forget that the sun is a star too.

These thoughts inside,
the ones I try to hide

these
terrifying
memories
casually
colliding
nearly
dying
constantly
reminding
me

that I'll never truly be free
of this deep depressing misery

~~that you left me.~~

There's this coping mechanism
I have inside my head.

It shutdowns before danger,
like the senses are heightened
and I'm just the passenger,
on this nightmare ride, I'm stuck on
not knowing if I will survive
this mental ache phenomenon.

I drop before things go down
blackout before the sirens sound,
as I can only go so far before it's too late
beat myself up for my own mistakes.

So this coping mechanism I made,
will be the brick wall to my escape
and keep me safe
from my own *earthquakes.*

You said I was playing victim,
but you didn't realise
that you were playing
killer.

The sound of thunder
doesn't affect her,
she waltzes with danger
but spins with caution,
as she knows the steps
but drowns in emotion.

She gives her all every time
which often leads to her decline,
leaving others feeling like she's the fault,
creating this cycle of mayhem and revolt.

The screaming inside
can't justify
her reasoning for anger,
I guess she's like a boat
without an anchor.

Find Me In The In-between

We're all a villain in someone's story,
trying to get in the way of their glory.

For you can't be the hero in everyone's scene
or their leading princess in their dreams.

You have to accept you're bad in someone's eyes,
their lover in disguise,
the one who came along and made them realise
that they told their sweet little lies
to recover from their demise
and achieve their sinful highs.

While they pushed you aside,
you were the one who compromised
but yet you're left feeling brutalised
and somehow come out looking like the bad guy.

However,
it gives me peace to know
that I was set free
and if she ever asks about me?

Make sure you paint me as
the marvellous villain in your history.

Find Me In The In-between

Bravery is;

walking into flames
and coming out the other side
realising
you always had it in you
to burn
and come back again.

For the moments
that make you want to run
and the moments just before,
for every second that I'm waiting
for you to walk out my door.

Is it mad to think that you could be different
and somehow make it through?
the twists and turns of my labyrinth
that make its way back to you.

So here's to dreaming
you're not like the others
here's to hoping you'll always be here,
for every good and bad story
every smile of mine and every tear.

You see countless others left and ran,
so I will forever be praying
that you'll be
a better man.

I had to sit there and listen to him
break my heart

as if

It wasn't the hundredth time
that I had heard it
that summer.

A tall glass of everyone's favourite,
slowly intoxicating
trying to savour it.

Guitar in hand, indie poster background
falling asleep to the sound
of lovers in the night
and friends in the light.

It's like the stars become you
how little time I get to spend in your view,
flying past me every time we meet,
friends that can only handle
so much heat.

Before we collide
brushing aside the consequences
of ruining this version of us we adore,

I guess we've never crossed that line before.

Find Me In The In-between

I could see the way

you carried your addiction,
your words held such contradiction.

The glass in your hand
shaking
as you hid the pills you were taking

like I was so naive
to think you had it all under control

when I knew
I was just another distraction
for you to console.

I once believed love was hiding their secrets,
I once believed love was them being my only
weakness.

I once believed love was being just friends who
casually kiss,
I once believed love was only seeing them on a
monthly basis.

I once believed love was holding someone who wasn't
mine,
I once believed love was praying that next time they
would be kind.

I once believed love was finding a reason to talk to
them at school,
I once believed love was trying my best to keep my
cool.

I once believed love was screaming I love you down
country roads at 3 AM,
I once believed love was determined for me to find
them.

I once believed love was making promises in cities
that I can't step into anymore,
I once believed love was listening to the same song,
crying on the floor.

I once believed love was captured in four days,
I once believed love was me begging them to stay.

I once believed love was dancing in corners in the
dark,
I once believed love was knowing we would never be
apart.

I once believed love was trying to remember all the
things that they did right,
I once believed love was knowing that they couldn't
even stay the night.

I once believed love was all of these things before
however, now I can't be so sure.
I realise that they can't be true

because the one thing
I now believe love is,
is **you.**

My head rests against the pillow,
I heard you leave down the stairs below.

What nightmare have I just woken up in?
last night you were the killer who crept in.

Who gave you permission to take control?
leaving a woman feeling less than whole.

Where was the consent in this exchange?
a man who felt the need to take revenge.

You left her with false hopes
of a future already dismissed

and the pain you left
that will
always persist.

I still remember the hospital elevator
that brought me to somewhere
past hell.

The sight of you there
made me realise,
that I would take
every argument on the street
If it meant I never got to see you
in the depths of your defeat.

- heartbreaking hindsight.

The photographs tell me
you've changed,
you don't look like you anymore.

I tell myself I don't care
while I sit here
studying every detail
like I was there next to you.

- How social media kills me.

I got a
taste for it,
I felt your drizzle
touch my lips.
I remember how you
demanded to be known,
touching everything I called home.

You made way for new starts,
like my re-do for a broken heart
and you never missed a chance,
to kiss, to sing and to dance.

Wishing I could save it for another day
but all of this now just reminds me of yesterday
and when it starts, it all comes flooding back
filling the space like a forgotten soundtrack.

Funny how you think I'm talking about you,
because after all the pain,

I'm actually in love with the rain.

Why is love so life-threatening?

Is it because
we attach our hearts to moments
and when the moments
turn into just memories,
so does our heart.

It kills us from the inside.

- Something I wrote when I was sixteen.

Glass
is destined to break
you forget how easy it was
to take parts of me
and I'd happily sit there and listen to you scream
(It still haunts my dreams)

constantly running from a voice
that I can't quite drown out
making me doubt
that I'm stuck in this hole
of regret and sadness
and no matter what I do
I'm destined for madness.

It was inevitable what was at stake.
You
turned my heart to glass
and watched it break.

I saw you again last night,
with the twinkle of lost history in your eyes
like the years
had made you realise
that blaming me
for the days we misplaced

gave you a permanent **aftertaste.**

They say:

She can't hold relationships down
and she falls in love too quick.

She breaks her own heart so much
it makes her sick.

She will keep repeating herself
because she loves the way it hurts.

Adding more victims to her poetry
and only making it worse.

When the rumours turned true,
I knew it had to be you.

Paparazzi crowd your new ruse
and you're all over the news,
painted black and red
like a torn-down figurehead.

The trickle of a faint apology
ran from your lips
however, I didn't hear it
over our love apocalypse.

The terror in their eyes,
as they watched you dramatise
what I predicted came through
and the rumours they once knew?

were always true.

With your hands
around my neck
you pushed me down
and took a step,
like you had just committed treason
searching to justify your reason.

To even contemplate
that you're the giant
I'm trying to hide from,

stuck in this dangerous place
of being just another one
~~of your victims.~~

Because you were an artist
and I was your painting
and you decided that
I wasn't your
masterpiece
anymore.

It was you
who made my mind explode,
reprogrammed my body
with your secret code.

Made me follow down
the same road you took,
all because it fucked you up.

I forgot there's no rest for the wicked,
I guess it's the final crime you committed
It's a one-way train
and I'm the one
you bought a ticket.

Find Me In The In-between

Part II

The Future
is all the what ifs and maybes,
the endless nights of possibilities,
the paranoia that breaks you
and the wishing well
that lets you down too.

It's ever-changing
and a daunting task
and I will try anything to get back.

I couldn't keep you
from your destruction
but I'll keep my word
and all of our lost conversations.

- promises I still make for you.

She believed,
had faith,
took the leap
and never took too long to decide.

She made the changes,
embraced the new
and all along
she knew,
she didn't need to wait
to be rescued.

You'll rue the day you fell in love
with someone like me
a human hurricane
that's all that I will ever be.

I came into your life
and destroyed everything in my path
and didn't stick around for the aftermath
of the mess that I'm creating,
making you think that
I'm the one who's been waiting
for someone like you
to come along and enter my life.

When in reality,
I was the one holding the knife,
to this facade of a relationship that we've performed.

Leaving the audience wanting more and warned,
of a girl who would one day come along
and cause a disaster but you just ran and ran,
faster and faster, after her.

You see, I promise to love you
when you're in pain
as long as you love me
when I'm a human hurricane.

It's a delicate thing
believing,
when you've already
broken faith.

I often find myself
deprived of memories,
I didn't even commit.

like a past life that lingers
in the armchair where you sit
memories flashing out of time,
like the worn-out camera
lost at the parties
that used to be mine.

Dwelling on a past
and living in delusion,
I'm only guilty if it's proven.

I don't think
they even knew
what consent was?

If they did
they wouldn't have left this pain

that's still here
after all these
years.

I'm far away
further than the love that could have stayed
from the boy I didn't chase,
the time I didn't waste

and you're still in the same place,
the same depressed life you try to embrace
the memories you try to erase,
the job
the girl
the house you 'showcase'

but you'll never see past your own vanity,
If only you had an inch of humanity
you wouldn't be falling into this mundane insanity

and after everything we went through
you know what?
I'm happy for you.

Now I'm somewhere else across the sea

and I bet you still think about me.

I don't think I'll ever understand
the worth of the wait
and maybe
I'm not supposed to feel my world shake
or be there long enough
to hear
my belief system break.

I'll run every time
it even comes close to the end,
because I'm done

lying to myself

that the worth of the wait
is worth all of my mistakes.

I hope you're somewhere
resting in peace
because you'll always
be dead to me.

As crying lightning
fills her skies
what you fail to realise
is that girl in front of you dying,
is finally
surviving.

I'm here again

staring at the life you had

before me.

Jealous
of the people
who knew you, like I do.

Jealous
of the photos
that I'm not in
(like somehow I could have been)

and the green-eyed monster
having the audacity

to make me believe
like I'm any different
to those

before me.

Too many times
I've been told to
stop
standing up for what I believe in
be a woman that can
'hold it all in.'

but how can that be possible
when this fire
that burns inside of me,
will never be put out
by your
insecurities.

Go slowly
with me now
I don't know how to react
you're unlike anything I pictured,
but you keep my eye contact.

Here we go again,
how quickly I whispered
 "I'm yours"

the dancing,
the feeling of flying
you swiftly became my cure.

Navigate this world with me,
take me by the hand,
show me how to live again
and change
all my future plans.

I forever left you
finding loopholes
in your future stories
and wondering how different
they would be
if they were
with me.

In every quiet moment,
In every corner, we touch
I'm reminded of
what it's like to be free

knowing that you are my lighthouse
when I'm lost at sea.

Just like a throat punch

I had this
gut-wrenching hunch

that this wouldn't last

So I will breathe in,
while I have the right

and see you in hindsight for the rest of my life.

Just because
you didn't witness my trauma,
doesn't make it
any less real.

I'm sick and tired of
bystanders thinking they know it all

when **oblivion**
doesn't even come close.

Maybe

we were just a

spur of the moment

and this version of us

will forever be frozen.

You taught me how to be loved the right way

but I didn't even have it in me to stay.

Years have dawned

and I'm still sitting here

begging you to let

bygones be bygones,

as I was just a girl

trying to move on.

I often find times
to thank the sun
as it is a constant reminder
that even you,
can rise
and fall too.

I know I'm not easy,
I never promised I would be.
I'm all or nothing
and never found in the grey

either you'll let me leave or you'll let me stay.

Just give me your time,
If that's all I ask of you
and just love me for as long as you can,
I know it's a daunting task
that others couldn't do.

How is it
that fate brought us together
right on time

as if

I hadn't been waiting my whole life.

Questions your children will ask someday

who's in the forgotten photos?
who's in the receipts you enclose?

who became the chaos you couldn't lose?
who's in the memories you try to excuse?

who gave you the love you still hold true?
who came along and ruined
every single one after too?

who's the girl you still blame for all your pain?

Please tell them my name.

I vowed from that day
not to cry anymore
over long-lost history.

I felt like I had to rip up
all the books I have ever studied
because none of them
had taught me
us.

How hopelessly wonderful
it is to get your
heartbroken
then
mended again
by your friends.

- All along that was the real love you needed.

Too good

to be anyone's part-time,
like glitches in the system
when we crossed the line.

Yet I'm still here rooting for you,
like a cheerleader, you can turn to
when other girls
are in your line of sight,
waiting for when the moment is right,
to kiss her, breathe her in
happiness is when we both win.

Take back our prizes,
revel in the compromises
as I don't want
what we have to end
I'm just happy
I get to be your friend.

They asked me

if I'm spiritual

I said

"I'm on my knees every day"

I once believed that eyes tell stories,
but his,
I didn't see one in particular.

It's like,
I saw my life in bookcases,
in future bedtime conversations

to *our* grandchildren
and I wanted to hear
every single damn one of them.

"Some people like chasing storms."

She turned to me and said
as we were winding down the country roads

"I don't know, I think I'd survive a hurricane."

Find Me In The In-between

Part III

Courage to wait,
courage to change,
courage to accept
and courage to let go.

Leading to this key moment
where I lost myself in twenty-seventeen
and now here lies where I am now
in
The In-between.

I have a theory
that every poet is heartbroken,
forever writing the words
that were unspoken.

Forever time capturing
the monumental pain,
hoping someone will come along
and mend it again.

For it's the poets that suffer the most
from the words we hold so close,
the memories we imprison,
the story already unfolded and written.

On our pages that release,
our restless souls
trying to find
peace.

You were the collateral damage
I made along the way,
caught in the eye of the storm
I gave you a reason to stay.

I was a mess on a comedown
from a catastrophic process
that I found myself in,
alone and depressed.

I didn't care about anything or anyone
and It's the truth I can't take back from.
Those years are all a haze you see,
memories I can't even fathom into reality.

The girl next to you
was nothing like me
and I regret that I let myself
treat you badly.

This is my apology.

- A letter to the others.

The teenager trapped inside
painted how she wanted
the one
to look like

but life isn't how we plan
and I was too young to understand
that the heart you held
in your hand
was already breaking
by a broken man.

Every year there's this weight I carry,
that you'll have new years
without me,
the countdown to midnight is that guarantee.

The years go on
and time has healed all wounds
and I know you're out there somewhere
healing too.

The past no longer counterfeits
and with every moment
leading to midnight
I'll count like my life depends on it.

Perhaps you don't think about it at all
and perhaps you didn't hold me gun to the wall.

The drinks were thrown,
you wanted to be alone
but I watched as everything I've ever known,
walk out of the scene,
~~(once again finding herself in the in-between)~~

Their faces were real,
like I had just received
the golden seal of approval
from your foes,
their hidden applause
as everyone knew that the curtains
were about to close.

I could have stayed,
but instead
I followed you down the country road
threw my heart down on the floor
and witnessed the fall.

Perhaps our hearts
aren't meant to be held against the wall.

Everyone knew
that the truth
in his crimes
was worth
her reputation
a thousand times

Don't believe the dreams you have at night,
they will jeopardise your ideals
and right before your eyes
play games with how you feel.

They will tell you what you want to hear
showing up like memories
except it's been years
that quickly turn themselves
into seconds of your biggest fear.

You have the power to take it all away
but they stay and when pressed,
you decide to breathe in the time you have left,
because by morning,
they are gone without warning.

So don't believe your dreams,
please
as I know now,
It's the only place you get to see me.

Find Me In The In-between

<u>Only you notice the little things</u>

like
how I bite my tongue or play with my fringe
or how my shoulders never sit still.

How I'm always thinking of the future
and the people I left behind,
how our memories play over and over
and how I wish that time could rewind.

It's like your mind prioritises,
the way I breathe
and the colour of my sleeves
and how many days it's been
since you last saw me.

It's like you see my world in yours
and I hope you know that
I've never needed anything more.

Wishing we were still friends

as if

It wasn't me who left.

Yeah maybe
we were buried in the drama
and all we saw was karma,
because you were asking for too much
held my heart that was already crushed.

I've escaped from the secrets and lies,
the way you locked eyes
like no one had the keys to
yeah, maybe
that's the only love you're used to.

Yeah maybe
I preferred it when it was chaotic,
but love isn't about begging you to 'stop it'
I learned from the love that let me go,
more thankful than you will ever know.

Yeah maybe
it was just me being naive,
and you weren't a bad person,
you were just 19.

If it's not in this world
then let it be the next

As I've come to accept
that I'll never know when
I'll be able to hear your voice
say

hello again.

Even after all these years

I keep telling myself to stop defending them.

For years I justified,
why I had to defend their honour, ego and pride.

When it's them,
who pushed me aside
and took the breath right out of me.

Which made me realise that,
love isn't meant to be
protecting their worst habits.

Love is about finding someone
who understands it.

- *A message from a survivor.*

She,
who is thunder on a good day,
the rain I desperately needed,
came into my life,
subdued my existence and succeeded.

For it was her
who showed me my wildest nights,
cured me of my heartbreak
and taught me to believe in what is right.

She was unlike any other,
an unbreakable mess,
but she was mine and it's about time I confess.

That she was sweet like honey,
the softest lips I have ever felt.

Consumed me on the dance floor,
I was the bee and
she watched me melt.

Everyone
fell for the devilish stare
the charming smile and sexual flare.

Everyone's favourite wingman
and partner in crime
couldn't stop me
from warning the next in time.

Heart like armour,
he finds a way to charm her,
as everyone flocks to his grin
his wondrous ways to let you in.

But you're only his friend
and you can't keep
waiting for the weekend.

As I sit here
I can't help but
count
the five hundred days of summer
I had experienced
that year.

But just like my favourite movie,
that I rewatch,
a thousand times

that summer,
for all it's worth
will always be mine.

The music stopped,
my heart dropped.

I watched the world pause
before us
like fate had to warn us
before us
not knowing what to expect
before us
a future about to arrive
before us
our worlds finally colliding
before us
our past loves
before us

The music stopped
why?
because I never knew love
before us.

So I will meet you
at

Chapter One

again

and maybe this time we can be friends.

Find Me In The In-between

It was easy to say you were to blame,
that I was the innocent pawn
in your chess game.

This love wasn't what we were used to,
so consumed in passion in secret rooms.
I led you down the stairwell and watched
as we signed our promises
with our fingers crossed.

You were hated so much by my rage,
you were missed so much by my rib cage.

You were rose-tinted by my eyes,
you were forgiven by my heart for your lies.

You were burnt in the flames of my spiral
and you are still tormented by my survival.

Just know that wherever you are today
I can hold my head up and say
that above all,
you were loved.

You had this certain look in your eye

"We could never have met"

like you were telling yourself
that the universe
must
have sent me
to you.

Why did no one tell us,
that a heart could wound and scar?

Did you grasp mine
and sense a distant dying star?

You know I wouldn't blame you
for realising it was over,
you still stuck around
to witness the Supernova.

You watched it burn,
long enough to detonate
found your fallout shelter
and didn't have long to wait.

Despite the time difference
I think we both know,
that you still feel my tremors
from years ago.

Alone

in this world

that I know so well

between

bittersweet peace

and

heartbreaking hell.

You were the kindest soul
I had ever known,
please don't believe for one second
that you were ever alone.

I believe soulmates
are people who don't leave
and that the bond between us will never end.

I'm so lucky

- that I get to call you my best friend.

The bench outside engraved
'We have cracked the midnight glass'

like it was trying to tell me my fortune
before I stepped into that room,
the room that led me to you.

You who I didn't see coming,
You who I had told myself didn't exist.

Fate really did,
step up that night
and I will celebrate by
cracking the midnight glass
for the rest of my life.

"I would have drunk the centuries away with you"

just to make you feel anything
other than sadness.

<u>Airports</u>

"have always been my drumroll"

I remember the strange look in your eyes
like I was crazy to think
a place filled with people and delays
I find peace and a reason to stay.

They are the moment just before a kiss

or the eager Christmas Eve bliss,
or the person you're still waiting to meet,
or the cafe with your favourite empty seat.

They are the gateways
to our next adventure,
so kiss me in every single one of them
like we've never been apart,
and get ready to hear
the banging drum
of my heart.

Find Me In The In-between

Why I secretly hate birthdays:

the ruined nights
the drunken fights

Every year the same insight,
(as we turn a year older)
realising all the happiness
I still owe her.

Tears fill the same cups,
just another year of self-destructs.

Too afraid to move on
and
too scared to admit

that you never want
this year to end
or to ever repeat it.

I've always been one to look for arrows,
to search for my yellow umbrella.
I always had a tiny hope
that fate would come waltzing in

but I lost all faith in fairytales.

I stopped believing
that I needed to be saved
and one day
I no longer looked for the yellow umbrella
or arrows along the way.

I took the train
I drank wine like champagne
(like I was already celebrating)

because I took my chance

and all it took was for you
to reach out your hand
and ask her
to dance.

I will remember
to keep storytelling
in the waiting

If it's all I have,
then I will sacrifice myself on this hill.

The patience of a saint
has come to confess her sins,
with all her will.

So no matter what happens,
she will become clean
of the shadows of seventeen
and she will continue to live
within

the in-between.

Find Me In The In-between

Author Bio

Josie Eckersley is an English, Lancashire-born, Edinburgh-based author. A teacher by trade, she started writing poetry from an early age and has composed poems based on her own experiences in her life, over the last ten years.

In this debut poetry collection, 'Find Me In The In-between' She explores and represents themes of heartbreak, moving on and taking chances, hoping others will find comfort in knowing it's ok to find themselves in the in-between too.